Minibeasts

Paul Mason

Ask your parent/s or carer for permission before purchasing any of the creatures in this book to _____ ___ __ ___ do keep a _____ you keep it _____ ontainer.

Published 2011 by
A&C Black Publishers Ltd.
36 Soho Square, London, W1D 3QY

www.acblack.com

ISBN   HB 978-1-4081-3378-1
       PB 978-1-4081-3379-8

Text copyright © 2010 Paul Mason

The right of Paul Mason to be identified as the author of this work has been asserted by him in accordance with the Copyrights, Designs and Patents Act 1988.

A CIP catalogue for this book is available from the British Library.

This book is produced using paper that is made from wood grown in managed, sustainable forests. It is natural, renewable and recyclable. The logging and manufacturing processes conform to the environmental regulations of the country of origin.

Produced for A&C Black by Calcium. www.calciumcreative.co.uk

Printed and bound in China by C&C Offset Printing Co.

All the internet addresses given in this book were correct at the time of going to press. The author and publishers regret any inconvenience caused if addresses have changed or sites have ceased to exist, but can accept no responsibility for any such changes.

Acknowledgements

The publishers would like to thank the following for their kind permission to reproduce their photographs:

Cover: Shutterstock
Pages: Dreamstime: Sanja Baljkas 9, Miroslav Beneda 7, Dean Bertoncelj 19, Eric Isselée 3, 16, Kenneth Lee 1, 11, Xunbin Pan 20, Vladvitek 6; Shutterstock: Matthew Cole 14, 18, Steve Cukrov 21, EcoPrint 13, Eric Isselée 17, Cathy Keifer 4, 10, Dr. Morley Read 15, Audrey Snider-Bell 12, Johan Swanepoel 5, yxm2008 8.

Contents

Beasties are Best

Do you want a pet? You could choose a pet dog or a cat or...

Bugs aren't boring!
If you want a really exciting pet, pick a **minibeast**.

How about keeping a moth?

Roll up, roll up

Dung beetles like rolling poo into balls. Gross!

Pretty pet

5

Ant Farm

Pet ants live in a special house called an ant farm. You can buy one from a pet shop.

Keep a perfect ant farm

1 Add a little water each day.
2 Add a drop of sugar water every week.

Feed your ants apple and lettuce.

Two stomachs

Worker ants have an extra stomach. They store food in it to feed their babies.

Feed me

Grasshopper

Grasshoppers make great pets and are easy to keep.

Make a hopper house

1 Put some earth in a small fish tank. Spray with water.
2 Cover the top of the tank with **wire mesh.**

Don't let your grasshopper escape!

See me climb

Give your grasshopper stalks and twigs to climb up. Hop to it!

I'm off!

Praying Mantis

Warning – this pet must be kept alone. Put two together and they will fight to the death!

Make a mantis home

1   Fill a fish tank with leaves and twigs.
2   Cover the tank with wire mesh.

Feed your pet with **moths** and flies – tasty!

Yum, yum

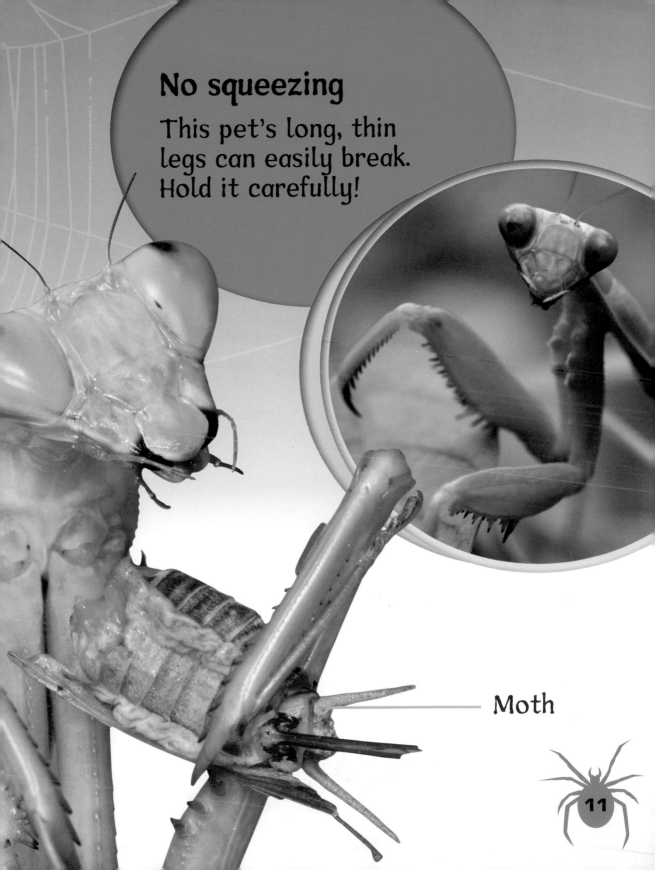

No squeezing

This pet's long, thin legs can easily break. Hold it carefully!

Moth

11

Scorpion

Scorpions have a sting in their tail, so choose this pet carefully!

Choose a scorpion

1 Pick a scorpion whose sting is not too **poisonous**.

2 Make sure your scorpion cannot climb the glass sides of its tank.

Claw

I'll sting!

12

Tail

Deep freeze

Scorpions can survive if they are frozen. They just **thaw** and walk away!

A scorpion has huge claws.

Spider

If you get a pet spider, make sure it cannot escape. Imagine the scream if your mum met it in the bath!

Keep a happy spider

1 Spiders love to spin **webs** on twigs and leaves. Put plenty in its home.
2 Give your spider lots of flies to eat. Tasty!

Spider children

Some spiders have up to 800 babies.

Keep a scary tarantula!

I'm really annoyed!

Spiny Leaf Insect

If you want a crazy-looking pet, this is the one for you!

Handle carefully

1 To pick up your pet, first you'll have to find it!
2 Hold your pet carefully. It is easy to break its legs.

Leaf insects look just like leaves.

Just for boys

Only male spiny leaf insects can fly.

Leaf me alone!

17

Centipede

If you like to handle your pet, do not get a centipede. They have a sharp bite!

Looking after a centipede

1 Keep it in a **secure container**.
2 Never scare a centipede. It will bite!

I'll bite!

Centipedes have lots and lots of legs.

Leg

Up all night

Centipedes hunt
for bugs at night.

Rhinoceros Beetle

A rhinoceros beetle can lift things that are 850 times heavier than itself! It's the world's strongest creature.

Keep a healthy rhino

1 Give it plenty of space. It loves to roam around.
2 Feed it with rotting wood and fresh plants.

Must fly!

On the go

Rhinoceros beetles love climbing. Make sure your pet has lots of twigs in its home.

Rhinoceros beetles are great flyers!

21

Glossary

minibeast fun word for insect

moths insects a little like a butterfly

poisonous harmful if swallowed or touched

secure container holder or box from which a minibeast cannot escape

tarantula large, hairy, and poisonous spider

thaw when something melts after being frozen solid

webs sticky nets that spiders make from silk. Spiders eat flies and other insects that they catch in their webs.

wire mesh net of wire threads with only small holes between them

Further Reading

Websites

Make your own minibeast at:
www.kenttrustweb.org.uk/kentict/content/games/minibeasts_v3.html

Find out lots of fun facts about minibeasts at:
www.learninghuddle.com/sample_minibeasts/mini_beasts_myths.htm

Places to visit

Natural History Museum
Cromwell Road, London SW7 5BD, UK
www.nhm.ac.uk

Books

I Wonder Why: Minibeasts by Karen Wallace, Kingfisher (2008).

Nick Baker's Bug Zoo by Nick Baker, Dorling Kindersley (2010).

Index